# PASSOVER
## A SEASON OF FREEDOM

Passover Preparations

a JEWISH HOLIDAYS book

# ṗASSOVER
## A SEASON OF FREEĐOM

## by Malka Drucker
### drawings by Brom Hoban

HOLIDAY HOUSE · NEW YORK

ACKNOWLEDGMENTS

THE AUTHOR would like to thank the following people for reading the manuscript and offering helpful suggestions: Rabbi Harold M. Schulweis, Rabbi Chaim Seidler-Feller, Vicki Kelman, and Margery Cuyler.

ABOUT THE PHOTO CREDITS:

Skirball is short for Hebrew Union College Skirball Museum, Los Angeles.

Yivo is short for "from the archives of the Yivo Institute for Jewish Research."

JTS is short for The Jewish Theological Seminary of America.




Printed in the United States of America

*Library of Congress Cataloging in Publication Data*

Drucker, Malka.
Passover, a season of freedom.

(Her Jewish holidays)
Bibliography: p.
Includes index.
SUMMARY: Retells the story of the Exodus and relates its meaning to the Seder meal and Passover preparations. Includes recipes, crafts, puzzles, and games for celebrating the oldest Jewish holiday.
1. Passover—Juvenile literature. [1. Passover]
I. Hoban, Abrom. II. Title. III. Series.
BM695.P3D78 296.4′37 80-8810
ISBN 0-8234-0389-0 (lib. bdg.)

For my grandfather,
MORRIS EPSTEIN,
who taught me the four questions.

# CONTENTS

# TO THE READER

*Pesach*, or Passover, the Jewish festival of freedom that comes in early spring, is the oldest and one of the most-loved holidays of the Jewish people. The highlight of the eight-day festival is the *seder*, an evening meal which recalls the *Exodus* of the Israelites from Egypt.

The dinner is full of unusual foods and customs. It was originally designed to make the participants, especially the children, curious about the meaning of Passover. The more questions and discussions, the better, because questions are a sign of thinking, caring and, most of all, freedom.

I hope this book, like the seder, will spark curiosity about what it feels like to celebrate Passover. A book can only suggest the taste of *matzah*, the melody of a song, and the excitement before Passover, but a personally experienced seder may bring you closer to understanding why this three-thousand-year-old holiday is still celebrated with joy and hope by Jewish families all over the world.

9

An Egyptian Pharaoh

# I
# BREAKING OUT

*Let my people go!*

EXODUS 5:1

WHEN the children of Israel first came to Egypt 3,300 years ago, they were not a nation or a people. They were just a large hungry family looking for a place to feed their flocks of sheep. Their relative Joseph, a valued adviser in the court of *Pharaoh*, Egypt's king, had invited them to settle in nearby Goshen. Within a generation the Israelites became a prosperous, hard-working part of Egyptian society. They were different from the Egyptians because they spoke Hebrew and worshiped one God instead of the many Egyptian gods, but Pharaoh let them live as they chose.

By the time Joseph and Pharaoh died, hundreds of Israelites lived in Egypt. A new Pharaoh came to power who had not known Joseph and who mistrusted his family. Fearing that its wealth and large population would give the Israelites—or Hebrews, as they were also called—the strength to rise up and

11

join Egyptian enemies, he tried to weaken them by reducing their numbers.

First, he ordered the Hebrews to leave Goshen to help the Egyptians fortify the cities of Pithom and Raamses against any attacks. He ordered the Israelites to mold bricks of clay and straw and to build pyramids with the bricks. The Israelites gradually became Pharaoh's slaves. He was sure that sixteen-hour work days in hot fields would weaken their bodies and break their spirits. They would not have the strength to create children, and their population would dwindle.

The Israelites, however, still bore children despite their hard labor. Pharaoh took harsher measures and separated husbands from wives during the week. This also did not work, because the Hebrew women foiled Pharaoh by visiting their husbands each day, supposedly to bring them lunch. In this way they continued to become pregnant and bear children.

Pharaoh suspected that there was something strange about the way these people kept multiplying, and he feared them. When one of his astrologers told him that some day a male Israelite would rise up and free his people, Pharaoh wanted every Hebrew male infant to be killed. The midwives, women who helped at childbirth, were secretly ordered to take the newborn sons from their mothers immediately after birth and throw them into the Nile River. They were to tell each mother that her baby had been stillborn.

Despite Pharaoh's command, however, Israelite boy infants continued to survive. Pharaoh sent for the midwives and demanded an explanation. Appealing to his hatred of the Israelites, the midwives lied and told him that the Hebrew women, unlike the delicate, refined Egyptian women, were like animals. They had their babies quickly and hid them before the midwives arrived. The truth was that the midwives had been secretly saving these babies because they could not bring themselves to kill them.

Now Pharaoh dropped his shrewd and sly ways and told all Egyptians to drown every newborn Israelite boy in the Nile. Egyptians went into houses where they suspected a baby boy was being hidden. They brought along their own babies and pinched them to make them cry. When the hidden Hebrew baby heard the Egyptian babies' cries, he would cry, too. Then the Egyptians would take away the Hebrew boy.

Amram, a Hebrew, was worried that his wife, Jocheved, might give birth to a son, so he told her that they should have no more children. They would have to be satisfied with their only child, Miriam. But Jocheved protested, saying that Amram was worse than Pharaoh because he wanted to eliminate *all* Hebrew babies, not just sons. She convinced Amram to have another child, who turned out to be a boy. Jocheved hid her baby as best she could, but at three months he was too lively to be kept hidden. So she wove a basket of bulrushes, sealed the inside with tree sap to make it float, covered the inside with soft blankets, and put the baby into it. She hoped that the basket would float long enough on the Nile for someone to take pity on the baby and rescue him.

Miriam took the basket to the Nile and placed it near the river's edge. Then she hid in the bushes to see if anyone would rescue her brother. Before long Pharaoh's childless daughter came to bathe and heard the baby crying. Guessing immediately that it was a Hebrew child, she lifted it from the water. At that moment Miriam appeared and asked the princess, "Shall I get a Hebrew nurse to care for this child for you?"

"The Finding of Moses" by Paolo Veronese

The princess agreed and Miriam ran home to get Jocheved.

"Take this child and nurse it for me, and I will pay your wages because I've always wanted a child," Pharaoh's daughter told a relieved and joyful Jocheved.

When the baby was three and no longer needed to be nursed, Jocheved brought him to Pharaoh's daughter. She called him her son and named him Moses, which the rabbis translated as "I drew him out of the water."

Although Moses was loved and treated well in Pharaoh's palace, he remembered his mother and never forgot that he was an Israelite. It hurt him to see his people so harshly treated. One day he walked out to the fields where the Israelites were building a pyramid. There Moses saw an Egyptian taskmaster whip an old man for working too slowly. Moses was so enraged that he struck and killed the taskmaster.

Moses' moment of anger ended his life of privilege. If the Egyptian soldiers caught him, he would be executed. So Moses fled to nearby Midian. There he married Zipporah, a Midianite shepherdess, had a son, Gershom, and lived the quiet peaceful life of a shepherd. He worked for his father-in-law, Jethro, a Midianite priest, and was far from the troubles of the Israelites in Egypt.

One day while taking care of his sheep, Moses sat down and looked at the lovely hills surrounding Midian. Suddenly he caught sight of a thornbush burning more brightly than any fire that he had ever seen. He turned his eyes away at first, and then looked again. The bush was burning, yet it was not burning up. Moses heard a voice call, "Moses! Moses!"

Moses answered, "Here I am." The voice told him to remove his sandals because the ground upon which he was standing was holy.

When the voice said, "I am the God of your father, the God

of Abraham, the God of Isaac, and the God of Jacob," Moses hid his face. He was terrified. But he stayed and listened to God tell him to be His holy messenger. God had heard the groans of the Hebrews and wanted to rescue them by leading them from Egypt into a new land that flowed with milk and honey. "Come, therefore," God said, "I will send you to Pharaoh, and you shall free My people, the Israelites, from Egypt."

But Moses hesitated. "Please, O Lord," he replied, "I have never been a man of words; I am slow of speech and slow of tongue." He feared that neither the Hebrews nor Pharaoh would listen to him. Pharaoh didn't even believe that the Hebrew God existed.

God dismissed his protests. "Who gives man speech? Who makes him dumb or deaf, seeing or blind? Is it not I, the Lord?" God assured Moses that He would tell him what to say, and that Aaron, Moses' brother, could speak for him. It would be God's power, not Moses' power, that would persuade Pharaoh and convince the Hebrews. After all, God chose the lowly thornbush to represent Him when He spoke to Moses.

Moses returned to Egypt with his wife and son. When he went to see Pharaoh to tell him that the God of Israel wanted His people to leave Egypt, Pharaoh refused. Not only did he refuse, but he made the lives of the Israelites worse. He ordered them to make bricks, but he no longer gave them straw. They had to find straw and somehow make the same number of bricks as before. The exhausted Israelites blamed Moses for the extra work.

They told him that they didn't want his help. Even though their lives were terrible, they were managing to survive. They didn't know if Moses could give them a better life.

Moses would gladly have given up his job of being God's messenger, but God would not let him. To reassure Moses and his reluctant followers, God described in four different ways how He would help them:

1. I will free you from the burdens of the Egyptians.

2. I will deliver you from their bondage.

3. I will redeem you with an outstretched arm and through extraordinary chastisements.

4. I will take you to be My people, and I will be your God.

"Pharaoh is stubborn," God told Moses. "He refuses to let the people go." Moses would have to convince Pharaoh that there was only one God, whose might was greater than anyone's, including Pharaoh's. It would take "extraordinary chastisements," ten plagues, each more terrible than the next, before Pharaoh would relent.

The plagues were the consequence of Pharaoh's cruelty. Of all sins, the rabbis believed slavery was the most hideous because being master over another human being was the same as trying to be God.

Moses warned Pharaoh that God would turn the water of the Nile into blood, and that it would smell and be undrinkable. But Pharaoh didn't heed his warning. So, for seven days, the Nile was turned to blood, the fish were made to die, and the people had to dig frantically for water. Pharaoh thought it was no more than a simple magic trick that his own magicians could have performed. He refused to let the Israelites go.

In the second plague, God made frogs infest everything from food and beds to people's clothing. This time Pharaoh told Moses if his God could get rid of the frogs, Pharaoh would let the Hebrews leave. Moses gladly replied, "So that you know that there is none like the Lord, the frogs shall retreat from you and your people; they shall remain only in

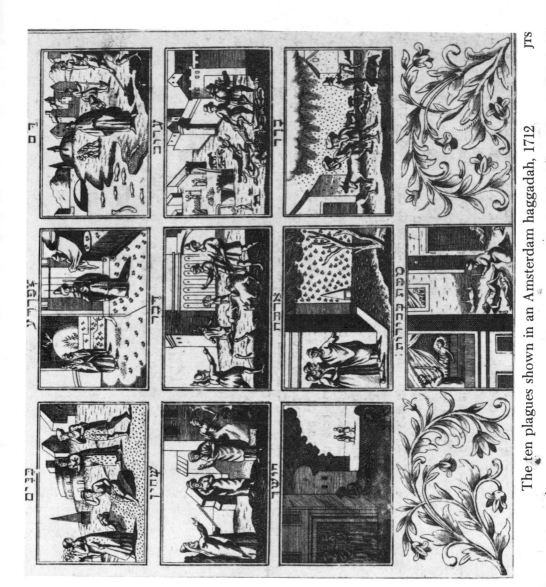

The ten plagues shown in an Amsterdam haggadah, 1712

JTS

the Nile." But, once the frogs had disappeared, Pharaoh took back his promise and became stubborn again.

For the third plague, God sent lice to every animal and person so that they itched horribly. Pharaoh's magicians were frightened and said it was the finger of God, but Pharaoh was unmoved.

So God sent a fourth plague—swarms of buzzing flies over Egypt. But he didn't send them to Goshen, where the children of Israel lived. Again, Pharaoh promised to let the Israelites go if the flies left Egypt but, as soon as they were gone, he changed his mind and hardened his heart.

Then, in the fifth plague, God infected and killed all the livestock in Egypt, except for those of the Israelites. Still Pharaoh would not let the Israelites go.

God then sent a sixth plague, which caused every human being and animal in Egypt to be covered with painful skin boils. But Pharaoh's heart remained hard.

God sent a seventh plague—heavy hail with thunder and lightning that killed all living things that were left outdoors, everywhere but in the land of Goshen.

Now Pharaoh began to be afraid. He summoned Moses and begged him to tell his God to stop the hail. He would free the Israelites. Moses stopped the hail but again Pharaoh changed his mind.

The Lord sent an eighth plague, and locusts covered the land so thickly that they made a black moving carpet over Egypt. They ate all the trees and filled the palaces and houses. When they were done eating, nothing green remained. Again Pharaoh begged Moses to get rid of the plague, and again he changed his mind when the plague was past. Pharaoh refused to learn his lesson.

The Exodus, shown in a Viennese haggadah

Then, in a ninth plague, God laid a dark fog across Egypt that was so thick that none of the Egyptians could see each other. God protected the Israelites, however, giving them light. As soon as Pharaoh told Moses he could have his wish, Pharaoh went back on his word another time.

The tenth plague was the most dreadful of all. God warned that He would take the firstborn animal or person from every house if Pharaoh would not free the Israelites. Slaves and kings would suffer equally.

God told Moses to tell each Hebrew family to prepare to flee that night. They were to pack up their belongings, slaughter a lamb, and take its blood to mark the doorposts of their houses. Then they were to roast the lamb and eat it hastily with unleavened bread. The Angel of Death would "pass over" the marked houses.

The Israelites knew by the crying all around them that the Angel of Death was near. When Pharaoh lost his only child, he called Moses to the palace and told him to take his people out of Egypt immediately. After 200 years of slavery, the Hebrews—the *Torah*, the holy books of Jewish learning, say there were 600,000 people—left Egypt guided by a bright, full moon. They took their cattle and whatever they could carry, including dough that hadn't had time to rise. Their suffering had united them as a people, with Moses as their leader.

Their misery wasn't over yet, however. Once again Pharaoh changed his mind and sent his soldiers to stop the Israelites. As the Hebrews got to the Red Sea, they heard the thunder of Pharaoh's army behind them. They were afraid that they would drown in the sea or be slaughtered by the soldiers. Miraculously, a strong wind came up to part the Red Sea, and the Israelites walked on the floor of the sea with walls of water

The crossing of the Red Sea

on either side. After they crossed safely, the water closed and the Egyptians drowned.

Before a baby is born, the sac that protects the embryo breaks and fluid flows from the mother. In the same way, when the waters of the Red Sea broke apart, the Jewish people were born. That is why the Exodus is the most important event in Jewish history. It is celebrated at Passover, which takes its name from the time God "passed over" the Israelite houses and spared the firstborn.

Although the holiday recalls the bitterness of slavery, its message is one of hope. The Israelites began as slaves, but they became a free people. How you begin is not as important as what you become.

"The Search for Leavened Bread" by Bernard Picart

# 2
# SPRING CLEANING

*For lo, the winter is past,*
*The rain is over and gone;*
*The flowers appear on the earth;*
*The time of singing is come.*

SONG OF SONGS 2:11

PASSOVER begins on 15 *Nisan*, at the first full moon of spring. The festival is celebrated for seven days in Israel and for eight days by many Jews outside of Israel. The difference in days has to do with the Jewish calendar, which is partly based on the moon.

Every holiday is determined at the beginning of the month by the appearance of the new moon. Twenty-two hundred years ago the rabbis sent runners to announce the new month. When all the Jews lived near Jerusalem, there was no problem in knowing what day the holidays would fall upon but, when the Temple was destroyed and the Jewish people were scattered over the world, the runners could no longer reach all the people before the beginning of the holidays.

Since the new moon can occur on the 29th or 30th day of the month, the rabbis made sure the holiday was celebrated on the right day by making most festivals outside Israel last two days. This is why many Jews in the United States hold seders at Passover on the first two nights. The first two days and last two days of the holiday are full holidays that are celebrated at home and in the synagogue. Many Jews don't go to school or work on those days, either. The four days in between, during which work can be performed, are called *Hol ha-Mo'ed* and are half-holidays.

Besides celebrating the Exodus and the birth of the Jewish people, Passover celebrates spring. Just as God freed the Hebrews from Egypt, so spring frees the earth from winter each year. From the first green shoots of barley that break the earth's cold surface to the first calves that break out of the womb, spring is a time of freedom and birth.

Passover also marks the beginning of the harvest season. The *omer*, a sheaf of barley, was brought to the ancient Temple in Jerusalem on the second day of Passover. This offering began "the counting of the omer." The Torah instructs Jews to count the omer from the second day of Passover until *Shavuot*, the fiftieth day. Decorative omer calendars, some of which can be colored in daily, help Jews keep track of the days. Because Passover is so rich with meaning, it has several names: *Hag-ha-Pesach*, Festival of the Paschal Lamb; *Hag ha-Matzot*, Festival of Unleavened Bread; *Hag ha-Asib*, Festival of Spring; and *Zeman Herutenu*, Season of Our Freedom.

A violin virtuoso plays so gracefully that it seems as though playing the violin is easy, but it takes years of training and preparation to create an effortless concert. Passover is like that too. It is a holiday of freedom, but it requires special preparation. Getting ready for the holiday is as much a part of the holiday as the holiday itself. The month before Passover is a time of cleaning, planning the seder, cooking, giving to the poor, and studying about the holiday. Everyone in the house knows that Passover is coming.

Food is more central to Passover than to any other holiday, and the most important Passover *mitzvot* or rules are about eating. For the eight days of Passover, Jews are not to eat or own any *hametz*, which means leaven. Hametz can be one or more of the following five grains mixed with water for eighteen minutes or more: wheat, rye, barley, oats, or spelt. Jews must also get rid of any food that is made with these grains, such as cookies, bread, pretzels, and bagels. Even the dishes and cooking utensils for leavened bread are considered hametz.

Eastern European Jews, from whom most American Jews are descended, take this a step further and do not eat corn, rice, or peas. Many Jews do not eat prepared food such as ice cream, cheese, or soda unless it is marked *Kosher le-Pesach*, or Kosher for Passover.

Hametz is not eaten so Jews will remember the haste of the Israelites when they left Egypt. They did not have time to let their bread dough rise. *Matzah*, the unleavened bread they ate, was the plain, humble bread of slaves.

Leavened bread is also puffed up and fancier than matzah and symbolizes self-importance. Passover is a time to remember the simplicity of the poor and to examine oneself for signs of being puffed up with too much pride. Eating matzah is a reminder that it's better to be flat and humble than blown up with self-importance.

"The Seder Meal" showing paschal lamb; late 18th-century Venetian engraving

Not eating hametz is easy, but ridding the house of hametz is a major project. More than just throwing away bagels, it is an exercise in changing an everyday house into a special Passover house.

The preparation of the house became important 2,000 years ago after the Temple in Jerusalem was destroyed by the Romans in 70 C.E. Before that time, Jews traveled from their villages to celebrate Pesach in a joyous, crowded Jerusalem. There they would buy a lamb to remind them of the paschal lamb sacrificed by every Hebrew family on the night of the Exodus. The lamb would be brought to the Temple to be slaughtered by the priest as a special sacrifice for Passover. It would be eaten at a seder on the first night of Passover.

After the Temple was destroyed, people wondered how they would celebrate Passover. Without the Temple, they couldn't have sacrifices or the high priests. The holiday survived because Passover became a family event with the home as the holy place instead of the Temple. The seder meal with its prayers replaced the sacrifices, and the participants at the seder, ignorant or educated, became the priests.

The kitchen is the busiest room in the house at Passover. The search for hametz begins there. Many people take their leavened food and give it to the poor. Others put it all in one cupboard and tape the door. Some Jews take this a step further and sell the hametz to a non-Jew. Because it is a complicated arrangement, a rabbi usually arranges the contract and sale. Although the food is not moved, the non-Jew has the right to take possession of it. After Pesach, the Jewish family buys back the food.

Searching is important at Passover. The holiday begins by searching for hametz, includes a hide-and-seek game at the seder, and requires a search for those who have no money for a seder. The poor are invited to seders and are given money by the synagogue from *ma'ot hittim,* a fund to meet the Passover needs of the poor. In Eastern Europe, the synagogue always provided a meal for the poor, but not on Passover. It was the family, not the synagogue, that bore the responsibility of the homeless.

Once the hametz is removed from the house, certain dishes and utensils which are used just during Passover are brought into the kitchen. They do not have to be fancy but, because they are used just once a year, they seem special. They are also a reminder of the delicious food placed upon them each Passover. Any dishes that are used all year that will also be used at Passover are sterilized. The kitchen is scrubbed until it shines. Many people cover the working surfaces with plastic or aluminum foil. The idea is to make everything new and fresh for the holiday, to use nothing that has touched hametz.

Sterilizing the Passover dishes

Some families do a thorough spring cleaning. Bedding is aired, shelving paper is changed, and the closets are cleaned. Old clothes and toys are given away.

Getting ready for Passover involves hard work, but it is also exciting. If it becomes a dreaded chore, the special feeling of the holiday gets lost. It helps if everyone in the family shares in the preparation.

The synagogue is less important than the home during Pesach, but does have special Torah readings and prayers for the holiday during the daily morning, aftenoon, and evening services. From the fall harvest holiday, *Sukkot,* in October, to Pesach, a daily prayer for rain is said. At Pesach the prayer becomes a prayer for dew *(tal),* because Israel, a dry country, depends upon early morning moisture for a good harvest. Because spring is a time of love, the romantic *Song of Songs (Shir ha-Shirim)* is read on the Shabbat during Hol ha-Mo'ed. It is also an expression of God's love for Israel. Only half the psalms of thanksgiving are chanted because the holiday is not completely joyous with the memory of the drowned Egyptian soldiers.

The Sabbath before Passover is called *Shabbat ha-Gadol*, the great Sabbath. Until rabbis gave weekly sermons, this was one of the two days of the year that they gave a speech. It is still a special Sabbath, with the rabbis answering last-minute questions about the laws of Passover and pointing out important themes of the holiday.

Because the firstborn Hebrews were saved in Egypt, the firstborn children were originally supposed to fast the day before Passover. This Fast of the Firstborn (*Ta'anit Behorim*) was too hard, however, since there was much work the day before the holiday. So the rabbis decided that, instead of fasting, the firstborn would attend a *siyyum*, a ceremony that celebrates the completion of a book of study in the *Talmud*, a commentary on the Torah, with a festive meal. Study, always

PHOTO BY IRVING I. HERZBERG

Airing the bedding in New York

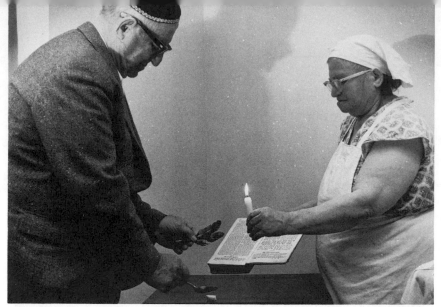

Bedikat hametz

an important mitzvah, is considered more important than this fast.

By the evening before Passover, everyone may feel worn out from what seems like turning the house upside down, but there is also a good feeling in knowing that the house is now as sparkling fresh as springtime. *Bedikat hametz*, the last-minute search for hametz, gives a final stamp of approval to the house. This ceremony is done on the evening before the first seder. (If the first day of Passover is on the Sabbath, it is conducted on a Thursday evening.)

After all the cleaning it's not likely anyone is going to find hametz but, since a blessing is never said in vain, ten pieces of bread are saved for the ceremony. The pieces are hidden by children around the house: on a windowsill or anywhere there could possibly be hametz, including a bed or a car. It's important to remember exactly where the pieces are, because you don't want to have bits of hametz around after the search.

A wooden spoon, a feather, and a candle are the traditional tools of bedikat hametz. Once the hametz is hidden, the lights are turned off and a blessing before the search is said. (See

Appendix.) Then the candle is lit and the children lead the father or mother to where the hametz is hidden. This is done in darkness and in silence. Someone sweeps the crumbs with the feather into the spoon. When the family finds all the pieces, they put them in a paper bag and say another blessing. (See Appendix.) The next morning the ten pieces, along with any hametz from breakfast, must be burned before eleven o'clock. The family declares in English, Yiddish, or Hebrew that any hametz in their house is now ownerless.

Although you may not eat bread after the Bedikat hametz ceremony, you also may not eat matzah until the seder that night. This is to whet your appetite for the matzah, to make the first bit of matzah a treat. Until sundown there is nothing left to do except the last-minute seder preparations.

Burning the hametz      PHOTO BY IRVING I. HERZBERG

Seder plates

# 3
# A FULL TABLE

*On Passover Jews eat history.*

Israel Zangwill

IF THERE is just one holiday that a Jew celebrates or keeps as a memory, it is Passover because the seder, with its drama and playfulness, is a wonderful family event. Members of the family and friends who have been away all year often return just for the seder. It becomes a lively reunion—sometimes with as many as fifty people—of grandparents, cousins, aunts, and uncles. Besides celebrating freedom, spring, and the birth of the Jewish people, Passover celebrates the power of the family to keep the Jewish tradition alive. The seder is a time machine that takes the family through 3,300 years of history. With prayers, songs, and food, the seder helps each Jew to relive the bitterness of slavery and the joy of being free.

The seder table is beautiful but unusual. At first glance it looks as though it's set for a dinner party but, in addition to the special dishes and flowers on the table, there are many other

Ornate seder plate

things. Even though it is an evening celebration, there is a place set for the youngest child. This is because children are central to the seder, since the ceremony is designed to teach them about the Exodus. The children also have a special place because they suffered the most when Pharaoh ordered the death of male infants.

A pillow rests on the chair of the leader, the person who conducts the seder. He or she sits at the head of the table. The pillow is not to prop up a tired leader but, rather, to symbolize freedom. A free person can be comfortable and recline, while a slave can never relax. A relaxed posture expresses a freedom of spirit.

Instead of food on each plate, there is a book. This is a sign that the party will be more than just a dinner party. It will be a talk-feast, almost a play, where people can be free to question, learn, and exchange ideas.

In front of the leader's place is a large ornate plate that displays five important symbols of Passover. First, there are small white bits of a root, which look deceptively mild. These are *maror*, or bitter herbs, eaten to remember the bitterness of Egyptian bondage. The power of the herb, which is often horseradish, is astounding. Romaine lettuce is also used as maror, because at first it tastes sweet, and then it turns bitter. In the beginning, the Israelites' life in Egypt was sweet, and then it turned bitter.

The next object on the plate is a brownish, unappetizing-looking mixture called *haroset*. This mixture is also deceptive because it is delicious. It is supposed to look like the mortar that the Israelites used to build the cities of Pithom and Raamses. Made of apples, nuts, cinnamon, and wine, its sweetness represents the promise of a better world. The mixture is also a reminder of the apple trees under which Israelite women bore their children, away from the eyes of the Egyptians.

The shankbone of a lamb, called the *zroah*, lies beside the haroset. This symbolizes the lamb eaten in haste when the Israelites fled Egypt. The shankbone is used because "the Lord, our God, brought us forth with a strong hand and an outstretched arm." The bone is a reminder of the arm.

Next to the shankbone is a roasted egg, called the *beitzah*. It is a symbol of the animal sacrifice that was brought to the Temple for each festival. The egg is also a symbol of life. One *midrash*, or legend, draws a connection between the egg and the Jews. Just as an egg gets harder as it cooks, so the Jewish people grew harder the more tyrants throughout history tried to weaken them.

Last, there is *karpas*, fresh greens that are usually parsley, celery, or lettuce. This is a symbol of new life in nature and the new life for the Jewish people when they were freed from slavery. It is also a hopeful sign because, just as spring follows winter and brings new life each year, so Jews hope that

"The seder table." On the seder plate, you can see (clockwise from foreground) karpas, a shankbone, celery, salt water, haroset, a hard-boiled egg, and an Elijah's cup. Also note the hagaddot, matzot, candlesticks, and wine glasses.

freedom will follow slavery for those who are not yet free. Beside each place is a dish of salt water, in which the karpas will be dipped. This is a reminder of the tears shed by the Israelites. It is also salty like the Red Sea and the waters of childbirth.

Next to the seder plate is a plate which holds three matzot, two for the blessing and one which will be broken by the leader as part of the ceremony. Two whole matzot are blessed because, when the Jews were in the wilderness, God gave them a double portion of *manna*, their survival food, on the Sabbath and festivals. The three matzot also represent the three remaining tribes of Israel—the *kohen, levi,* and *yisrael.* Because all Jews belong to one of these groups, it is as if the entire community of Israel sits at the seder table.

Of all the Passover symbols, matzah is the most important and, like the other symbols, it means several things. Matzah is the bread of slavery but, in addition, it is the bread of freedom because, at the seder's end, it symbolizes the paschal lamb.

Matzah also recalls a time of simplicity when additives like leavening weren't necessary. It is a natural food, a reminder that less is more.

The book at each plate is called a *haggadah*, which means "the telling." It tells the story of the Exodus, and is a guide to the seder. The first haggadah was written 1,000 years ago, when the rabbis feared that the story and the seder would be forgotten. Since then, 3,000 different editions have been written, each filled with history, literature, legend, folktales, and songs. Artists and writers have been inspired by the holiday to create beautiful haggadot, each with slightly different interpretations. All add to the richness of the holiday.

It is interesting that in the haggadah there is a detailed telling of the misery of slavery, the ten plagues, and the miraculous flight from Egypt, but that there is not a word about Moses. Passover is a celebration of the Jewish people, not of Moses. Moses was a great leader, but he was only God's messenger. His presence assured people that God needed human beings to perfect the world, but it was God who freed the Israelites, not Moses. Because the rabbis were afraid that the people would make Moses into a supernatural being, which would confuse the meaning of the Exodus, they left him out of the haggadah.

German 19th-century matzot cover

THE ISRAEL MUSEUM, JERUSALEM

A page from a haggadah illustrated by Ben Shahn, ca. 1945

At each place setting, including the children's, there is a cup for wine. Four times during the seder, wine will be poured from several decanters on the table. The number four recalls God's four promises of freedom to Moses. At Passover, wine helps everyone celebrate freedom by being joyful and happy.

There is one cup of wine at the center of the table that stands alone. This is the cup of *Elijah*, the prophet who, according to Jewish teaching, will announce the coming of the Messiah. Elijah is also the helper of the poor. In hundreds of legends, he appears at the last moment to save a starving family. Because of Elijah's two tasks, the rabbis said that the Messiah will come when there are no hungry people in the world. Each year at Passover, everyone carefully watches Elijah's cup to see if he has come to drink the wine and bring us closer to the promise of a better world.

Despite all this preparation, the seder table is still not complete. It needs the family, from the oldest to the youngest, to make these lovely but lifeless objects holy.

Bohemian 19th-century crystal Elijah's Cup

THE ISRAEL MUSEUM, JERUSALEM

"Passover Night" by Raisa Robbins

# 4
# A GREAT BIRTHDAY

*And you shall explain to your child on that day,*
*"It is because of what the Lord did for me*
*when I went free from Egypt."*

EXODUS 13:8

For 3,000 years, Jewish families have celebrated Passover with variety and creativity. Each family, contributing its own customs and style, has given the holiday its richness and depth. There is no one way to conduct a seder and no rabbi to lead the service. It is up to the family to make the seder, and the choices are endless. Family members pick which of the dozens of haggadot to use, or they write their own version. Within the haggadah, they choose which parts to include and which parts to skip. Some families make the two seders different; the older children may conduct the second seder, or they may hold it outdoors, just as the early seders were celebrated in the wilderness. From choosing the menu to deciding who will lead the seder, there are questions and decisions. This is important, because a free person makes choices. Seder means order. It is the sequence of the evening's events, but it also sparks new ideas and individual expression.

Jewish learning is a partnership between what once happened and its meaning today. It isn't enough just to learn the facts of the Exodus—it needs to become part of you. The seder provides the chance for people to bring their imaginations to the ceremony. What does it feel like to be a slave, to see your parents forced to do degrading work, or to be left as a baby to float down the Nile? What would you have done if, like Moses, you had seen a taskmaster beating a slave? The evening ceremony begins by reliving slavery and ends by imagining what the world will be like when all people are free.

The haggadah describes the fourteen steps of the seder. The first step is the lighting and blessing of the candles at sundown. (See Appendix.) Candles, with warmth and brightness, signal the beginning of the holiday. All Jewish holidays begin with candle-lighting at sundown because, just as winter comes before spring and slavery comes before freedom, so darkness comes before light.

The leader pours each person's first cup of wine and recites the *kiddush*, the blessing for the Sabbath and holidays. (See Appendix.)

The leader sometimes wears a *kitel*, a white robe, which is a reminder of the clothes worn by the high priests in the Temple. White also symbolizes gladness and freedom. Everyone else at the seder is dressed up, often in something new to mark the freshness of the season.

After the kiddush, a pitcher, bowl, and towel are passed around the table for the hand-washing. Since this is not a washing of hands before a meal, no blessing is said. Instead, this ceremony makes everyone feel like priests because the high priests in the Temple washed their hands before all holy duties. The leader holds up the karpas—perhaps a sprig of parsley—and gives everyone a bit of it. Before eating, the participants recite a blessing to thank God for the earth's food and to remember that we all share the responsibility of keeping the world a healthy place for growing things. (See Appendix.) Then the karpas is dipped into the salt water and eaten. This custom is at least 2,000 years old. Since karpas is really an hors d'oeuvre, some families also eat such foods as potatoes, eggs, or carrots. Otherwise, the time between karpas and dinner could be long and hungry. The rabbis encouraged everyone to dwell at *length* on the telling of the story.

*Yachatz*, the breaking of the middle matzah, follows karpas. The other two matzot on the matzah plate are left alone. With a loud crack, the leader breaks the middle matzah in two

European ceremonial seder towel for hand washing, about 1800

THE JEWISH MUSEUM

Seder table

Bokharan child reading a question aloud from a haggadah

and folds a soft napkin around the larger of the two halves.
The wrapped piece is a reminder of the dough the Israelites
carried in knapsacks when they left Egypt. It is also a reminder that the poor never eat a whole portion; they must
always save something for later. The leader puts the smaller
piece between the two whole matzot, but is is the larger piece
that interests the children. They watch very closely where the
leader puts it. It is the *afikoman*, which means "dessert." The
children steal and hide the afikoman—this can happen any-
time during the seder. The afikoman is also a substitute for the
paschal lamb that was sacrificed before the Temple was destroyed.

The leader lifts the plate of two-and-a-half matzot and says,
"Behold the matzah, bread of the poor, which our ancestors
ate in the land of Egypt. All who are hungry, let them come
and eat. All who are in need, come and celebrate Passover
with us." These words started the tradition of families inviting
homeless or newly immigrated Jews to their seders.

The story of the Exodus is started by a child, not by the
leader. The youngest person at the table asks the leader four
important questions. The questions are concerned with how
this night is different from all the others in the year. For the
youngest child, the greatest difference is that, for one wonderful moment, everyone listens to him or her. First the questions
are asked in Hebrew, and then they're repeated in English. For
the child reciting the questions, getting ready for Passover
often means learning how to say these questions in Hebrew:

1. Why is this night different from all other nights? On all
   other nights we eat either leavened or unleavened bread;
   why, on this night, do we eat only matzah, which is unleavened bread?

2. On all other nights, we eat vegetables and herbs of all kinds; why, on this night, do we eat bitter herbs especially?
3. On all other nights, we never think of dipping herbs in the water or anything else; why, on this night, do we dip the parsley in the salt water and the bitter herbs in haroset?
4. On all other nights, everyone sits up straight at the table; why, on this night, do we recline at the table?

These are the four traditional questions, but others may be asked by anyone at the table. Different questions may even be substituted. An Israeli haggadah written in 1942 asks this question: "When will peace reign in our land and in the entire world?" This is still a good question. The leader responds by saying "We were slaves in Egypt." This is the beginning of the story in which these questions are eventually answered. The story is often interrupted with questions and discussion.

The rabbis knew that, because there are different kinds of people, there must be different ways of telling the story in order to make it understood. The haggadah describes four kinds of children.

The first child is a wise child who loves the holiday and wants to know all about it. The whole story and the meaning of the Passover customs are read out loud to him.

The second child is a scornful child. He does not understand what Passover has to do with him and asks, "What does this service mean to *you?*" By using the word "you," he separates himself from the Jewish community. This child is told that he would still be a slave in Egypt, because he does not consider himself part of the Jewish people.

The third child is "simple." He wants to know what Passover means but can only ask one question, "What is it all about?" He is told a short version of the story.

The fourth child does not sense that there is something

different about Passover. This child is the most ignorant of the four, because he does not even care enough to ask questions. He is also given a shortened version of the story.

Everyone at the seder understands these children, since a little bit of each child is in every person.

The ten plagues are remembered at the seder with sadness. As each plague is read—blood, frogs, lice, flies, cattle disease, boils, hail, locusts, darkness, death of the firstborn—everyone' dips a finger into his or her cup of wine and spills a drop from the cup. The seder is a joyful celebration, but some joy must be spilled because the Egyptians suffered too.

After this reflective moment, everyone sings a rousing *Dayenu,* a song of gratitude. Dayenu means "it would have been enough." If God had worked only one of his wonders, if He had only freed us and had not given us the Torah, it would have been enough. There is a blessing over the wine and the second cup is drunk.

The leader leaves the table for the hand-washing before the meal and recites a blessing. (See Appendix.) This is a good

JTS

The four children, from a Viennese haggadah, 1823. From right to left, you can see the child who does not know enough to ask questions, the simple child, the scornful child, and the wise child.

Immigrants celebrating Passover at Ellis Island, April 28, 1913

time for the children to steal the afikoman. No one really knows how this part of the Seder began. Some believe its purpose, like much of the seder, is to keep the children awake and curious throughout the evening. Others find deeper meanings to the hide-and-seek game. The hidden afikoman is like the mysterious order of the universe, waiting to be uncovered. Children hide the afikoman because everyone is a child in the search for the unknown.

When the leader returns he or she leads the blessings over all the food and the matzah. (See Appendix.) Then the leader breaks the matzah into bite-size pieces, one for each person at the table, and everyone eats a piece. The bitter herbs are dipped into the haroset and are eaten together after another blessing. (See Appendix.) The haroset softens the bitterness, but you still feel as though you're swallowing fire.

The last special food before the full dinner is the *Hillel* sandwich, named after the great Jewish teacher in the first century after the Common Era. The leader gives two pieces of matzah, with maror in between, to everyone. This sandwich combines the bitterness of slavery with the joy of freedom. Hillel wanted every Jew to remember the threat of slavery even in times of freedom and to keep the hope of freedom even in times of slavery.

The dinner is called *Shulhan*. At this point, everyone usually has an enormous appetite. There is no particular food that must be eaten, but the traditional meal may include hard-boiled eggs mixed with salt water, *gefilte* fish, matzah ball soup, turkey, sweet potatoes, fruit, tea, and cake. It's the most delicious meal of the year.

The leader must get the afikoman from the children to complete the meal and to continue the seder. The children have the upper hand in the bargaining because they know the seder cannot end without it. The leader offers a gift to the finder of the afikoman, and the discussion between the children and the leader may go some-thing like this:

LEADER: Where is the afikoman?
CHILD: What will you give me?
LEADER: A kiss.
CHILD: Forget it.
LEADER: What do you want?
CHILD: The Empire State Building.
LEADER: How about something a little smaller?
CHILD: A new baseball and bat.
LEADER: O.K. It's a deal. Let's have the afikoman and get on
with the seder.

The leader breaks the afikoman into little pieces and passes them around the table. Everyone takes a piece and eats it as dessert. It is the last food eaten at the seder. The afikoman was a good luck charm for Middle Eastern Jews. They thought a piece of it carried in a pocket would ward off illness and shipwrecks. Kurdish Jews bound a piece to an older son's arm and said, "May you be as close to your wife."

The first half of the seder focuses on the slavery of the past. The second half focuses on freedom and the hope of a better world some day. Joy, singing, and openness mark this part of the seder. The third cup of wine is poured and blessed. A child opens the door to welcome the prophet Elijah. Everyone hopes that Elijah will sip wine from his special cup and announce the coming of the Messiah. Jews believe that when the Messiah comes there will be no slavery, poverty, hunger, or war. People will live together in peace. The Messiah is supposed to appear as a poor beggar who will reveal himself when someone offers to share food with him. This is the message of Passover: that we will all be free when we are willing to share with one another.

A way to express this idea is to take Elijah's cup, which has been empty until this part of the seder, and pass it around the table. While the door stands open, everyone pours a little wine from his or her cup into the empty cup and sings *Eliahu ha-Navi (Elijah the Prophet)*. The idea is that this spirit of cooperation will bring the Messiah.

Opening the door for Elijah began for a frightening reason. In the Middle Ages a rumor spread that the Jews used the blood of Christian children for the Passover celebration. This blood libel, as it is called, was absolutely false. In fact, Jewish law considers blood impure. All blood from animals must be drained from meat before it's eaten. Still, ignorant people believed the rumor, so Jews opened the door at the seder to show that there was nothing about the ceremony to hide. They even drank white wine instead of red wine so that there would be no suspicion that they were drinking blood. Opening the door for Elijah began because of a lie, but became a gesture that expressed hope for a better world.

The fourth and final cup of wine is blessed and drunk with the toast, "Next year in Jerusalem!" When the Jewish people were scattered all over the world and couldn't return to Israel, these words had special meaning. Today it expresses the hope for a return to the holiness of ancient Jerusalem.

The seder ends with lively songs that praise God for leading the Israelites from bondage. Two of the most interesting songs are *Who Knows One? (Ehad Mi Yode'a)*, which tells, by number, the beliefs of Judaism, and *One Only Kid (Had Gadya)*, the story of what happens to a little goat. This funny song, sung as fast as possible, also suggests that justice is in store for all who try to crush other people and that, in the end, all of us are responsible to God.

חַד גַּרְיָא חַד גַרְיָא · דְזַבִּין אַבָּא · בִּתְרֵי זוּזֵי · חַד גַרְיָא חַד גַרְיָא :

ניקלין · חיין ליקלין · דט המט גירוסט חיין פעטרלין מוף גוויא ספֿעגע · חיין ליקלין חיין ליקלין

תָא שׁוּנְרָא · וְאָכְלָה לְגַרְיָא · דְזַבִּן אַבָּא בִּתְרֵי זוּזֵי · חַד גַרְיָא · חַד גַרְיָא :

קאמ דט קעטלין · חול מם רט ליקלין · רט דם המט ביקוסט מיין פֿעטרלין · חוט גוויא ספֿענע · מיין ליקלין · חיין ליקלין

וְתָא כַּלְבָּא וְנָשַׁךְ לְשׁוּנְרָא · דְאָכְלָה לְגַרְיָא · דְזַבִּין אַבָּא · בִּתְרֵי · חַד גַרְיָא · חַד גַרְיָא :

קאמ דט הינטלין · חול ביס רט קעטלין · רט דם המט גנעטין רט ליקלין · רט דם המט ביקוסט · מיין פֿעטרלין · מוס ספֿעגוג · מיין ליקלין · חיין ליקלין

נָא חוּטְרָא וְהִכָּא לְכַלְבָּא · דְנָשַׁךְ לְשׁוּנְרָא · דְאָכְלָה · יָא · דְזַבִּין אַבָּא · בִּתְרֵי זוּזֵי · גַרְיָא · חַד גַרְיָא :

קאמ רט טטעקלין · חול טלוג רט הינטלין · דז דם המט רט קעטלין · דט דם המט גנעטין רט ליקלין · רט דם המט קוסט מיין פֿעטרלין חול גוויא ספֿענע · חיין ליקלין ג[ו]

A haggadah page of "One Only Kid"

## WHO KNOWS ONE?
### *Last Verse*

*Who knows thirteen? I know thirteen!*
*Thirteen are the attributes of God;*
*Twelve are the tribes of Israel;*
*Eleven are the stars in Joseph's dream;*
*Ten are the divine commandments;*
*Nine are the months 'til childbirth;*
*Eight are the days 'til the covenant;*
*Seven are the days of the week;*
*Six are the volumes of Mishnah;*
*Five are the Books of Moses;*
*Four are the mothers of Israel;*
*Three are the fathers of Israel;*
*Two are Sinai's tablets.*
    *But One alone is our God,*
    *In heaven and on earth.*

## *ONE ONLY KID*

*An only kid! An only kid!*
*My father bought for two zuzim.*
*An only kid! An only kid!*

*Then came a cat*
*And ate the kid*
*My father bought for two zuzim.*
*An only kid! An only kid!*

*Then came a dog*
*And bit the cat*
*That ate the kid*
*My father bought for two zuzim.*
*An only kid! An only kid!*

*Then came a stick*
*And beat the dog*
*That bit the cat*
*That ate the kid*
*My father bought for two* zuzim.
*An only kid! An only kid!*

*Then came a fire*
*And burned the stick*
*That beat the dog*
*That bit the cat*
*That ate the kid*
*My father bought for two* zuzim.
*An only kid! An only kid!*

*Then came water*
*And quenched the fire*
*That burned the stick*
*That beat the dog*
*That bit the cat*
*That ate the kid*
*My father bought for two* zuzim.
*An only kid! An only kid!*

*Then came an ox*
*And drank the water*
*That quenched the fire*
*That burned the stick*
*That bit the cat*
*That ate the kid*
*My father bought for two* zuzim.

*Then came a slaughterer*
*And killed the ox*

*That drank the water*
*That quenched the fire*
*That burned the stick*
*That beat the dog*
*That bit the cat*
*That ate the kid*
*My father bought for two* zuzim.
*An only kid! An only kid!*

*Then came the angel of death*
*And slew the slaughterer*
*Who killed the ox*
*That drank the water*
*That quenched the fire*
*That burned the stick*
*That beat the dog*
*That bit the cat*
*That ate the kid*
*My father bought for two* zuzim.
*An only kid! An only kid!*

*Then came the Holy One, praised be He,*
*And smote the Angel of Death*
*Who slew the slaughterer*
*Who killed the ox*
*That drank the water*
*That quenched the fire*
*That burned the stick*
*That beat the dog*
*That bit the cat*
*That ate the kid*
*My father bought for two* zuzim.
*An only kid! An only kid!*

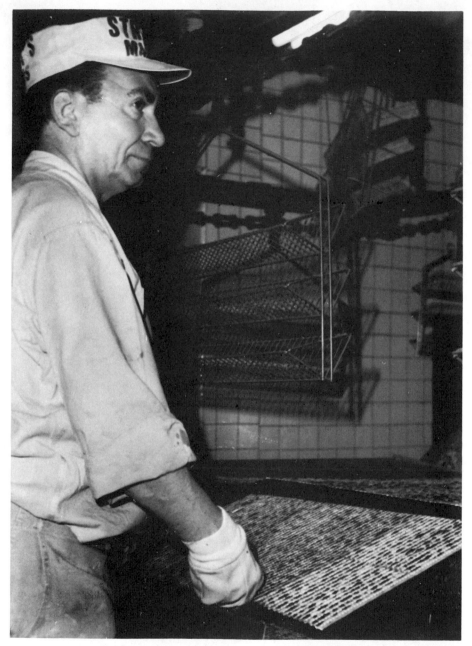

Finished matzah

# 5
# MATZAH BALLS AND MACAROONS

*All who are hungry, let them come and eat.*

PASSOVER HAGGADAH

PASSOVER gives you much to think about, but it also touches the senses. At the seder you see the spectacular table, hear the questions, songs and prayers, touch the shankbone and raise the wine cups, smell the spring flowers and fragrant dinner and, best of all, taste the special holiday foods. Even though many foods are forbidden, Passover cooking is a creative and delicious activity. Chocolate-covered matzah, macaroons, and just plain matzah smeared with jelly make it hard to pick which Pesach treat is the best.

No leavened bread may be eaten for the eight days of Passover, and unleavened bread, matzah, has to be eaten at the seder. Most people, however, like matzah well enough to eat pounds of it during the holiday. Although it began as a humble food, it has become almost magical the way it can

Matzah dough being rolled

taste so many different ways. Depending upon the recipe, it can turn into cake, cookies, pancakes, or dumplings.

Most matzah is made by machine now, but there are still a few factories that make handmade matzah in the same way it was made 150 years ago in Eastern Europe. First, an oven as large as a room, 10 feet (300 centimeters) by 14 feet (420 centimeters), is scrubbed free of hametz and made ready for Passover. Since fermentation takes place in eighteen minutes, the matzah dough must be mixed and rolled flat in a speedy fifteen minutes. Before the mixing, the flour and water are kept in separate rooms as a precaution against fermentation. Lines of workers quickly mix fresh spring water with carefully sifted flour in another room.

In still another room that is dark and cool to prevent light or heat from fermenting the dough, workers roll the dough into large pancakes and punch tiny holes into them with a special comb. This is also to prevent any leavening during the baking of the matzah. At the call "matzah!" the pancakes are draped on long sticks and put into the oven which is heated by coal and oak. With an expert twist of the wrist the pancakes fall off the sticks and lie flat in the searing 900°F. (500°C.) oven for thirty seconds. Each piece comes out with its own waves and shape.

It's not possible to make matzah at home because home ovens aren't hot enough, but there are many foods that you can make from matzah. The recipes in this chapter are simple, but they do require cooking or cutting, so it's a good idea to have an adult around while you're working.

PHOTO BY IRVING I. HERZBERG

Matzah "pancakes" going into oven

## ZWEIBEL MATZAH
### (An old, easy, and delicious snack)

*1 piece of matzah*
*½ an onion*
*pinch of salt*
*sweet butter*

Rub the matzah with the cut side of the onion. Salt the matzah lightly and put it in a preheated 300°F. (150°C.) oven for four minutes. Take it out and spread it with sweet butter.

Matzah brei is a breakfast or lunch dish that tastes something like French toast and scrambled eggs. It can be eaten plain or with sugar or jelly sprinkled over the top.

## MATZAH BREI

*4 matzot*
*4 beaten eggs*
*3 tablespoons butter or margarine*

Break the matzot into penny-size pieces and put them into a bowl. Pour water over the matzot and let the mixture

sit for a minute. Drain the water by putting a hand over the pieces as you pour the water into the sink. Press out all the excess water by squeezing the matzot in your hands. Melt the butter in a frying pan over a medium flame and add the matzot. Stir the matzot in the pan for a minute or two to toast it. Add the beaten eggs to the matzot, mixing thoroughly. Fry for three minutes, take off the stove, and eat at once. This recipe makes enough for four people.

Although matzah is flat and crispy, this recipe, made with matzah meal, makes puffy Pesach rolls. Matzah meal is ground-up matzah and can be found in food stores. Rolls are handy if you go to school during the middle days of Passover and carry your lunch, because egg salad is much easier to eat on a Pesach roll than on matzah.

## PESACH ROLLS

*1 cup water*
*1 stick of margarine*
*1½ cups matzah meal (375 milliliters)*
*5 eggs*
*pinch of salt*

Preheat the oven to 350°F. (180°C.). Boil the water in a saucepan. Add the margarine and salt. When the margarine is melted, pour the mixture into a bowl and add the matzah meal. Beat the eggs and add them to the mixture. Wet your hands with a little cooking oil or water and form balls the size of golf balls. Put them on a cookie sheet. Place the sheet in the oven and bake for thirty-five minutes. When the rolls are cool, cut them in half and spread them with your favorite sandwich filling.

Matzah balls, which are eaten with chicken soup, are a favorite Passover treat. Cooks guard their recipes closely and, the lighter the matzah ball, the harder it is to get the recipe. This recipe was generously given by an expert. It's foolproof but the cook advises, "Don't lift the pot cover while they are cooking."

## MATZAH BALL DUMPLINGS

*5 well-beaten eggs*
*6 tablespoons cold water*
*1 cup matzah meal (250 milliliters)*
*5 tablespoons rendered chicken fat*

Mix the ingredients together in a large bowl. Cover and put in the refrigerator for four hours. Bring four quarts of water to a boil. Roll the mixture into balls the size of golf balls, and drop into the boiling water. Cook *covered* for a half hour. The balls are then ready to be added to soup. This makes 10-12 matzah balls.

Macaroons are sticky cookies that, like all Pesach recipes, do not use leavening like yeast or baking soda.

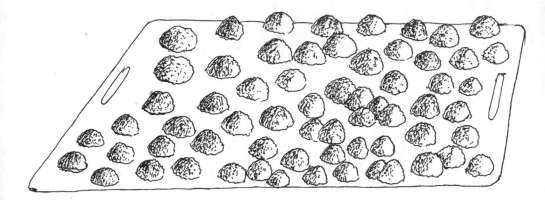

## ALMOND MACAROONS

*4 egg yolks*
*1 cup sugar (250 milliliters)*
*2 cups ground almonds (500 milliliters)*

Preheat the oven to 350°F. (180°C.). Beat the egg yolks well; add the sugar and beat until the mixture is lemon colored. Add the ground almonds and mix thoroughly. Chill for one hour in the refrigerator. Take small pieces of the mixture and shape into small balls. Place the macaroons on a greased baking sheet. Top with half an almond. Bake in the oven for ten minutes. This makes roughly 50 macaroons.

All these foods can be eaten year round, not just at Passover. Haroset, though, is a special Passover food. Its flavor is saved for the seder. Spread on matzah, its sweetness, a symbol of hope, blends with the ideal of freedom.

## HAROSET

*½ cup shelled walnuts (100 milliliters)*
*3 large apples*
*¼ cup sweet red wine (50 milliliters)*
*cinnamon*

Shell the walnuts and put them in a large bowl. Quarter and core the apples. Grind, chop, or blend the nuts and apples until they have the consistency of chunky peanut butter. Add a little wine until the mixture becomes like applesauce. Add cinnamon for flavor and refrigerate. Haroset tastes better when it is at least a day old, so it should be made the day before the seder.

Cleaning the house and changing dishes tells you that Passover is near but, when you make haroset, you know the holiday has arrived.

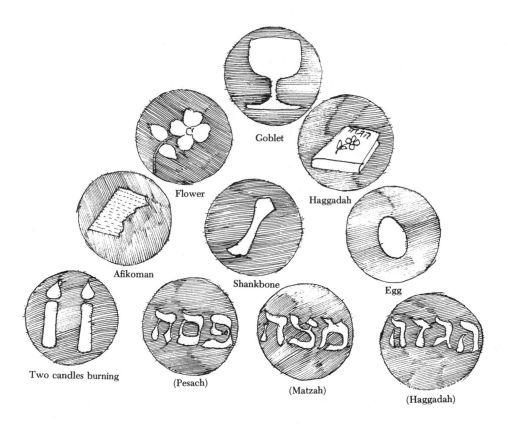

Goblet

Flower

Haggadah

Afikoman

Shankbone

Egg

Two candles burning

(Pesach)

(Matzah)

(Haggadah)

Craft symbols

# 6
# CRAFTS

*How is this night different from all other nights?*

PASSOVER HAGGADAH

CLEANING, cooking, learning about the Exodus, and learning the four questions are only part of getting ready for Passover. Making the house different by creating something special for Passover is important too. Crafts can be your "first fruits" of spring.

The rabbis discouraged showing off wealth but, on Passover, the home should shine with beauty. Just as spring adorns the earth, so this is a perfect time to adorn the house with splendid ritual objects.

Elijah's cup should look different from the other cups on the table. Here is an idea for an Elijah's cup that will make a colorful addition to the seder table.

## ELIJAH'S CUP

Take a clear plastic wine glass that can be found in party supply stores. You may have to buy several at a time, but they are inexpensive and can be used as gifts. Color the entire outside surface of the glass, stem included, with permanent felt-tip markers—you can draw figures also. When the cup is dry, spray the outside with a light coat of lacquer. Spray cans of lacquer can be found in hobby or hardware stores. When the lacquer dries, the plastic will be dull and look like delicate blown glass. Wash the cup by hand before using it. The inside should be clean and shiny.

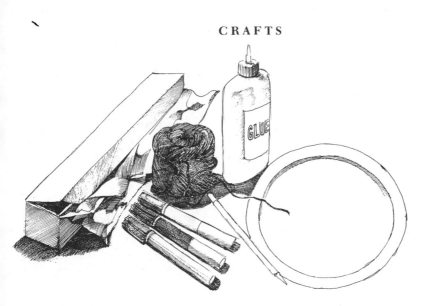

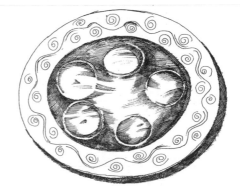

## SEDER PLATE

Another Passover necessity is the seder plate. Even if your family already has one, a few plates are helpful to allow everyone at the table to be near a plate. On a heavy 10½-inch paper plate (25 centimeters), use a pencil to draw five circles, 2 inches in diameter (5 centimeters), around the inside edge of the plate. These circles, which will hold the five symbolic foods, should be the same distance apart. Dip wool yarn in white glue and paste it around the rims of the circles. Then draw a design around the outside rim of the plate and glue more yarn to it. When the glue is dry, cover the plate, including the bottom, with aluminum foil. Press the foil down, so that the yarn underneath will make a pattern. Color the center of the circles and the outside rim design with permanent felt-tip markers. The finished product is a sparkling seder plate. If you want to use the plate for more than one seder, use nut cups to hold the food so it doesn't soil the plate.

Now you've made a wine cup for Elijah and a seder plate for holding parsley, a roasted egg, a shankbone, bitter herbs, and haroset. But how about something for the matzah?

## MATZAH COVER

Here is an idea for a fancy matzah cover that allows you to make your own design. The designs at the beginning of the chapter can be used for this project. Cut a piece of fabric 1 foot square (30 centimeters). It can be white, colored, or have a pattern, but the pattern should be small. Hem or sew a fringe to all four sides. Write the word matzah, in English or Hebrew, on an iron-on patch. The Hebrew letters should be 2 inches high (5 centimeters), the English letters 1 inch high (2.5 centimeters). You may need two patches. Cut out the letters and iron them onto the center of the fabric. Then choose designs from the beginning of the chapter, draw them on more iron-on patches, cut them out, and iron them onto the fabric.

## PASSOVER PILLOWCASE

The pillowcase upon which the leader reclines can also be
decorated. Put a piece of paper inside a solid-colored or white
case. Using the designs at the beginning of the chapter as a
guide, draw pictures on the case with felt-tip markers. The

paper inside the case will keep the ink from soaking through to the inside of the material. Since the afikoman is often hidden in the pillowcase, don't forget to draw an afikoman.

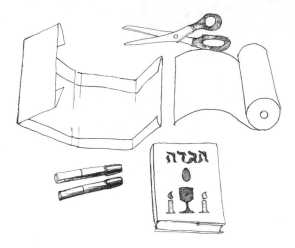

## HAGGADAH COVER

Haggadot get messy at the seder because of all the food that drops on them. You can protect the outside of the book by making a cover for it. Measure the haggadah and cut a piece of paper 6 inches longer (15 centimeters) and 2 inches wider (5 centimeters) than the book. Fold the paper according to the illustration. White butcher paper has a fresh clean look and is sturdy, but any heavy paper will do. Aluminum foil also makes a bright cover. Using felt-tip markers, write the Hebrew word for haggadah, הַגָּדָה , on the front or, if you're feeling particularly ambitious, try drawing the story of the Exodus in three scenes. The first picture could have slaves with pyramids in the background, the next picture Moses at the burning bush, and the last could show the Red Sea. Whatever you decide, the haggadah will be the better for it.

## PLACE CARDS

If you're expecting many people at your seder, it can get very confusing when everyone tries to find a seat at the table. Passover place cards solve this problem, because each person finds his place by looking for his name. You can make place cards from 3″ high x 5″ wide (7.5 x 12.5 centimeters) index cards folded in half, so that they become almost square. The cards come in several colors. With a dark or bright felt-tipped marker, write the person's name at the bottom of the card so that there's enough room left at the top for a design. You can use the designs at the beginning of this chapter or think up your own. Watercolors, crayons, and felt-tip markers all show up clearly on the cards. If you have a good supply of old magazines around the house, you can also decorate the cards with cut-out pictures of small flowers. Then your place cards will become a bouquet of people.

Children on the Lower East Side of New York playing nut games during Hol ha-Mo'ed

# 7
# PASSOVER FUN

*Rejoice in your festival, and you shall have nothing but joy.*

DEUTERONOMY 16:14

SEARCHING for hametz and finding the afikoman are only part of the fun of Passover. Here are some other games, with a few ridiculous riddles, to think about when you're grinding horse-radish, trying on new clothes to wear at the seder, or shaking matzah out of your clothes after the seder.

## JOURNEY

This is a good game to play between courses of the dinner. The leader begins by taking the afikoman and putting it on his shoulder. Someone asks, "Who are you? Where are you from? Where are you going? What will you take on your journey?" The answer goes something like this: "My name is Malka. I'm leaving Egypt to be free in Israel. I'm taking *apples* with me."

The person sitting next to the leader takes the afikoman, puts it on his or her shoulder and says the same thing, except the name changes and the person says, "I'm taking apples and *bananas*." The next person says "I'm taking apples, bananas, and *carrots*." The play goes around the table, with each person remembering what has been said before, and adding another food in alphabetical order. You can mention anything but hametz. It gets harder and harder as the list gets longer, and of course everyone laughs if you get mixed up or forget.

## NUTS

Nut games are played at Passover because they are an ingredient in haroset. Give each player an empty bowl, six nuts, and two pencils. In the first game, players try to see how many nuts they can pick up with the two pencils. The first player who fills his or her bowl with six nuts wins. The second game is more connected to Passover because it is a hiding game. One person hides a few nuts in one hand, and everyone else tries to guess how many nuts are hidden, or whether there is an odd or even amount.

## PASSOVER RIDDLES
(The answers start on page 80.)

When is a piece of wood like Pharaoh?

What is square, flat, and picks up pins?

How is the haggadah like the Red Sea?

What is flat, red, and bumpy?

When is stealing rewarded and not punished?

## CODE

This sentence reveals the hope and optimism of the Jewish people for 2,000 years. Can you decipher it?

13 22 3 7 — 2 22 26 9 — 18 13 — 17 22 9 6 8 26 15 22 14

## SCRAMBLED WORDS

These words have something to do with the meaning of Passover. Can you unscramble them?

THOASER
DROEMEF
ULEPGA

## WORD COUNT

How many words can you make from the letters of these words? (No proper nouns and no plurals.)

Passover
Afikoman
Shankbone

# ANSWERS

## RIDDLES

When it is made into a ruler.
A magnetic matzah.
They are both read (red).
A sunburned matzah.
When the afikoman is stolen.

## CODE

Next Year In Jerusalem! (z = 1, a = 26)

## SCRAMBLED WORDS

HAROSET
FREEDOM
PLAGUE

## WORD COUNT

*Passover*

| as | ape | apse | rave | posse |
|----|-----|------|------|-------|
| so | are | aver | reap | prose |
|    | ass | over | rope | prove |
|    | eat | pare | rove | spare |
|    | era | pass | save | spear |
|    | oar | pave | sear | spore |
|    | par | pear | soap | versa |
|    | pea | pore | soar |       |
|    | rap | pose | sore |       |
|    | sap | rape | spar |       |
|    | sop | rasp | vase |       |

## Afikoman

| am | fin | fain |
|----|-----|------|
| of | kin | foam |
| no | man | main |
|    |     | moan |

## Shankbone

| ah | ask | bank | shank |
|----|-----|------|-------|
| an | ash | beak | snake |
| as | ban | bean |       |
| be | hen | bone |       |
| ha | nab | home |       |
| he | one | honk |       |
| oh | sun | knob |       |
| on |     | none |       |
| no |     | sane |       |
|    |     | sank |       |
|    |     | snob |       |

# AFTERWORD

THE SLAVERY of the Israelites is not a happy or proud memory in Jewish history, but it has given the Jewish people sympathy for others in bondage. More than a historical recollection, Passover is also a reminder that there are still slaves in the world who need help.

Hillel said, "If I am not for myself, who will be for me? If I am only for myself, what am I?" On Passover, Jews pray that the festive meal and its memories will give them the strength to fight for freedom in the world.

# Appendix

Blessing before the search for hametz:

Praised are You, O Lord our God, Ruler of the Universe, Who has sanctified us with Your Commandments and enjoined upon us the mitzvah of removing leaven before Passover.

Blessing after finding hametz:

May all leaven in my possession which I have not seen or removed, be regarded as non-existent and considered dust of the earth.

Blessing after lighting the candles:

Praised are You, Lord our God, Ruler of the Universe, Who has taught us the way of holiness through Your Commandments which include the mitzvah of kindling the (Shabbat and the) Festival lights.

We thank You too, dear God, for keeping us alive and in good health so that we are able to celebrate this day.

Blessing for the Sabbath and holidays:

> Praised are You, Lord our God, Ruler of the Universe, Who has taught us the way of holiness through Your commandments. As a token of Your love, O Lord our God, You have given us (Sabbaths for rest), events for rejoicing, festivals and holidays for gladness, (this Sabbath day and) this Feast of Unleavened Bread, the season of our freedom from slavery in Egypt. You have quickened within us the desire to serve You, and in joy and gladness, have given us Your holy (Sabbaths and) festivals. Praised are You, O Lord, Who hallows (the Sabbath and) Israel, and the festivals.

Blessing over karpas:

> Praised are You, O Lord our God, Ruler of the Universe, Creator of the fruit of the earth.

Blessing over hand washing before the seder meal:

> Praised are You, O Lord, Who has sanctified us with Your Commandments and enjoined upon us the mitzvah of washing the hands.

Blessings over food and matzah:

> Praised are You, O God, Who gives us food from Earth. Praised are You, O God, Who has sanctified us with Your commandments and enjoined upon us the mitzvah of eating unleavened bread.

Blessing over maror and haroset:

> Praised are You, O Lord, Who has sanctified us by Your commandments and enjoined upon us the mitzvah of eating the bitter herbs.

# GLOSSARY

AFIKOMAN—The broken piece of matzah put aside at the beginning of the seder, which is eaten at the end of the meal.

BEDIKAT HAMETZ—The last-minute search for leavened bread before Passover.

BEITZAH—The roasted egg on the seder plate that symbolizes the ancient festival animal sacrifice.

C.E.—Common era. Christians use the term A.D., which means "in the year of our Lord," or after Christ.

ELIJAH—A prophet and helper of the poor who will announce the coming of the Messiah.

EXODUS—The second book of the Torah, which describes the departure of the Israelites from Egypt.

GEFILTE FISH—A mixture of boiled freshwater fish formed into balls.

HAGGADAH (haggadot, pl.)—The special book read at the seder that tells the story of Exodus and the meaning of the food on the table.

HAG HA-ASIB—Festival of Spring; another name for Passover.

HAG HA-MATZOT—Festival of Unleavened Bread; another name for Passover.

HAG HA-PESACH—Festival of the Paschal Lamb; a name for Passover.

HAMETZ—Leavened bread and food, as well as dishes and cooking utensils used throughout the year, that cannot be used at Passover.

87

Haroset—A mixture of apples, nuts, wine, and cinnamon eaten at the seder in remembrance of the mortar used by the Israelite slaves to build Egyptian cities.

Hillel—A great teacher and leader in the first century after the Common Era.

Hol ha-Mo'ed—The four middle days of Passover.

Karpas—Fresh greens, such as parsley, celery, or lettuce, used during the seder to symbolize springtime.

Kiddush—The blessing for the Sabbath and holidays, said over wine.

Kitel—a white robe that the leader wears during the seder.

Kosher le-Pesach—Food that is permitted during Passover.

Manna—The special food God gave the Jews when they were in the desert for forty years; probably a plant that enabled them to survive.

Ma-ot hittim—Money set aside for the poor for their Passover celebration.

Maror—Bitter herbs, often horseradish, eaten to remember the bitterness of the Israelites during Egyptian bondage.

Matzah (matzot, pl.)—Unleavened bread.

Midianite—A member of an ancient northern Arab tribe mentioned in the Torah.

Midrash—A story or legend that has its beginnings in the Torah; often it explains some part of the Torah.

Mitzvah (mitzvot, pl.)—A good deed; a rule or commandment that Jews believe was given to them to follow by God.

Nisan—The first month of the Jewish calendar.

Omer—A sheaf of barley.

Pesach—Festival of Passover.

Pharaoh—The ruler of ancient Egypt.

Seder—The order of the family ceremony on the first two nights of Passover.

Shabbat ha-Gadol—The Sabbath that falls before Passover, on which the rabbi gives a great sermon.

SHAVUOT—A holiday that celebrates the fruit festival in Israel, and which ends the counting of the omer.

SHIR HA-SHIRIM—*Song of Songs;* a love poem that is read in the synagogue during Passover.

SHULHAN—The seder dinner following the eating of the Hillel sandwich.

SIYYUM—A ceremony on the day before Passover in which the firstborn celebrate the completion of a book of study in the Talmud with a festive meal.

SUKKOT—A harvest holiday in which a branch house is built outside the synagogue or home.

TA'ANIT BEHORIM—Fast of the Firstborn that used to be practiced on the day before Passover.

TAL—Dew.

TALMUD—One of the commentaries on the Torah.

TORAH—The five Books of Moses that contain all Jewish Law; Old Testament.

YACHATZ—The breaking of the middle of the three matzot.

ZEMAN HERUTENU—Season of Our Freedom; another name for Passover.

ZROAH—A roasted shankbone; reminder of the paschal lamb sacrificed by the Israelites.

# SUGGESTED READING

THE celebrations and observances described in this book are mostly Ashkenazic, or Eastern European, the origin of most American Jews. There are other Jewish groups, however, who have different Passover customs. The Samaritans in Israel, for example, still roast a paschal lamb just as it was done 2,200 years ago. If you want to know more about Passover, the following books might be helpful.

Philip Goodman, *The Passover Anthology* (The Jewish Publication Society of America, Philadelphia, 1961)

Howard Greenfeld, *Passover* (Holt, Rinehart, and Winston, Inc., New York, 1978)

Richard Siegel and Michael Strassfeld, *The First Jewish Catalog* (Jewish Publication Society of America, 1973)

Morris Silverman, *The Passover Haggadah* (Prayer Book Press, Bridgeport, 1972)

*The Torah* (Jewish Publication Society of America, 1967)

# INDEX